Helen's Kitchen

Cookbook Favorites

Second Edition

Helen L. Shevel

Helen's Kitchen
Cookbook Favorites

Helen Shevel, now in her mid-eighties, is the mother of five, grandmother of eleven and great-grandmother of seventeen. She learned cooking, baking, crafting, home decorating and gardening from her Amish grandmother and her talented mother.

She has made this her life's mission. Winning numerous ribbons at County Fairs and other baking and cooking competitions, Helen now wants to pass on her favorite recipes to her children, grandchildren and her many friends.

Helen's Kitchen Cookbook Favorites Second Edition Copyrighted©2019 by
Helen L. Shevel

Printed in the United States of America

Second Edition

10 9 8 7 6 5 4 3 2

All rights are reserved. Only the recipes found in this book may be used or reproduced; no other content may be used in any manner whatsoever, including electronic or mechanical means, without written permission from the publisher or from Helen, except in brief quotations embodied in critical articles and reviews.

For information contact Baird Farms Publishing Co. in Mount Juliet, Tn.

www.wdjaq@aol.com.com

ISBN 978-1-945450-16-7

This book is dedicated to my five children, eleven grandchildren and seventeen greatgrandchildren, all whom brought me much joy and inspiration for this project.

H.

TABLE OF CONTENTS

Appetizers	pp. 3-9
Soups	pp.10-15
Salads	pp. 16-27
Breads	pp. 28-43
Casseroles	pp. 44-58
Entrees	pp. 59-67
Desserts	pp. 68-126
Miscellaneous	pp. 127-135
Index	pp. 136-138
Acknowledgements	pp. 139

MEASUREMENTS AND ABBREVIATIONS

c = cup

dz. = dozen

lb. = pound

oz = ounce

pt. = pint

pkg = package

qt = quart

T = tablespoon

tsp = teaspoon

" = inch

° = degrees

F = Fahrenheit Scale

APPETIZERS

Crab Tartlet with Lemon-Dill Sauce

2 T butter
1 T mayonnaise
2 T egg, slightly beaten*
1 tsp lemon juice, freshly squeezed
1 tsp Old Bay seasoning
1/8 tsp salt
1/3 c breadcrumbs (using day-old bread)
6 oz chunk crabmeat, drained
2 T green onion, thinly sliced
1 T pimentos, diced
1 T celery, minced
2 T heavy cream
1 pkg (15) Filo shells

*Lightly beat one egg; take 2 T for recipe

<u>Dill Sauce</u>
1 c mayonnaise
¼ c buttermilk
1 T fresh parsley, chopped
2 T fresh dill, chopped
1 T lemon zest, grated
2 tsp fresh orange juice
1 small clove of garlic, minced

Crab Tartlet with Lemon-Dill Sauce

1. Melt butter in a heavy skillet over medium heat.
2. Add onion, celery, and garlic. Sauté in butter for 3 minutes.
3. Remove from heat; add mayonnaise, egg, lemon juice, seasoning, salt, breadcrumbs, heavy cream and pimento. Mix thoroughly.
4. Gently fold in crab meat.
5. Use a small scoop to fill shells; place 1" apart on a parchment lined baking sheet.
6. Bake at 350°F for 20-25 minutes.

<u>Dill Sauce</u>

1. Combine all ingredients in a bowl and mix well. Chill. (sauce thickens as chilled).
2. Transfer 1 tsp sauce to each tartlet.
3. Garnish with lemon curls or dill sprigs as desired.

Jalapeno Poppers

3 dz. jalapeno peppers, cut in half lengthwise to remove seeds and membranes
8 oz mild Bob Evans sausage, browned and cooled
1 pkg (8 oz) cream cheese, room temperature
½ c sharp cheddar cheese, grated
1 pkg center-cut bacon

1. In a bowl combine cooked sausage, cream cheese, and cheddar cheese. Mix until well blended.
2. Spread open each pepper and fill each with approximately 1 T of mixture. Close pepper.
3. Wrap ½ slice bacon around each pepper. Place seam side down on a wire rack placed on a jellyroll pan. Bake at 350°F until bacon is done.
4. Serve warm if possible.

Poppers are good warm or cold.

Fruit Dip

1 c raspberry jelly, room temperature
1 pkg (8 oz) cream cheese, softened
2 tsp sugar

1. Using a mixer, combine jelly and cream cheese.
2. Add sugar and beat until well blended.
3. Chill and serve.

Brie en Croute #2

1 sheet frozen Puff Pastry
1 T butter
¼ c pecans or walnuts, chopped
1 (8 oz) small wheel of Brie
½ c raspberry jam
1 egg, beaten

Brie en Croute #2

1. Preheat oven to 375°F.
2. Defrost Puff Pastry for 15-20 minutes to unfold.
3. Melt butter in a saucepan over medium heat.
4. Sauté nuts in butter for 5 minutes or until golden brown.
5. Place nuts on top of Brie and spread jam on top of nuts.
6. Gently roll pastry to increase size by 2" in each direction. Brush with beaten egg.
7. Gently remove the coating from the Brie. Center the wheel of Brie on top of the pastry sheet. Bring all four corners of the pastry together above the Brie and twist slightly to form a "bundle".
8. Gather pastry with kitchen/cooking string and tie in a bow.
9. Work the pastry until satisfied with the "bundle" shape. Brush with remaining beaten egg.
10. Place "bundle" on an ungreased baking sheet and bake 20-25 minutes or until golden brown.
11. Serve plain or with top quality crackers.

Serves 8

SOUPS

Baked Potato Soup

4 (about 2 ¾ lb.) large baking potatoes
2/3 c butter
2/3 c all-purpose flour
¾ tsp salt
¼ tsp white pepper
6 c milk
1 c sour cream
¼ c green onions, thinly sliced
3 stalks celery, thinly sliced
1 c sharp cheddar cheese, shredded
bacon bits (optional)

1. Bake potatoes at 350°F for 65-75 minutes or until tender. Cool completely.
2. Peel and cube potatoes.
3. In a large saucepan, melt butter.
4. Stir in flour, salt, and pepper until smooth.
5. Gradually add milk. Bring to a boil; cook and stir for 2 minutes or until thickened.
6. Remove from heat. Whisk in sour cream.
7. Add potatoes, green onions and celery. Reheat.
8. Garnish with cheese or bacon bits. (optional)

Serves 10

Chili

1 ½ lb. ground beef
1 can (28 oz) diced tomatoes, undrained
1 can each (15 oz) kidney, pinto and black beans, rinsed and drained
½ lb. fully cooked Kielbasa, cut in small pieces
½ c onion, halved and thinly sliced
1 can (8 oz) tomato sauce
2/3 c hickory flavored barbeque sauce
¾ c water
¼ c brown sugar, packed
2 banana peppers, seeded and diced
1 T chili powder
1 tsp ground mustard
¼ c black coffee, liquid
½ tsp each, dried thyme, oregano and sage
¼ tsp cayenne pepper, flakes
1 clove garlic, minced

1. In a Dutch oven or soup kettle, over medium heat, cook beef until it is no longer pink. Drain.
2. Add remaining ingredients; bring to a boil.
3. Reduce heat; cover and simmer for 1 hour, stirring occasionally.

Serves 10-12

Taco Soup

1 lb. ground beef
½ onion, diced
1 can (15 oz) pinto beans
1 can (15 oz) black beans
1 can (15 oz) diced tomatoes
1 can (15 oz) hominy
1 can (10 oz) ROTEL diced tomatoes and chilis (mild or hot)
1 pkg taco seasoning
1 pkg Hidden Valley dressing
V8 juice if more liquid is desired.

<u>Garnish</u>
Sour cream
Mexican cheese
Tortilla strips

1. In a skillet, brown ground beef until done. Add remaining ingredients in order listed.
2. Cook on low-medium heat for 1 hour or until done.
3. Garnish with sour cream, Mexican cheese and tortilla strips as desired.

Serves 4-5

Ham and Bean Soup

3 qt cold water
1 small-medium ham bone
1 lb. baby lima beans
1 medium onion, diced
3 stalks celery, diced

1 medium carrot, diced
1 tsp salt
2 T chicken flavored bouillon, cubes or powder
¼ tsp fresh ground pepper
1 can (15 oz) diced tomatoes

1. Soak beans in water for 4-6 hours. Drain and rinse.
2. In large crock pot, place ham bone, soaked beans, onion, celery and carrots.
3. Add enough water to cover all ingredients and more.
4. Add salt, chicken bouillon, pepper and tomatoes.
5. Cook on low heat for 7-8 hours. Add more seasoning as desired.

A pan of corn bread goes well with this soup. H.

Butternut Squash Bisque

2 medium carrots, sliced
2 celery ribs with leaves, chopped
2 medium leeks, white portion only, sliced
1 jalapeno pepper, seeded and minced
¼ c butter
2 lb. (about 6 c) butternut squash, peeled, seeded and cubed
1 can (14 oz) chicken broth
½ tsp salt
½ tsp ginger
1 c half & half cream
¼ tsp white pepper
½ c pecans, toasted

1. In a large saucepan, sauté carrots, celery, leeks and jalapeno pepper in butter for 10 minutes, stirring often.
2. Add squash, broth, and ginger; bring to a boil.
3. Reduce heat, cover, and simmer for 25 minutes or until tender. Cool until lukewarm.
4. In a blender or food processor, puree squash mixture, in small batches, until smooth. Return to saucepan.
5. Add cream, salt and pepper. Mix well.
6. Heat through but <u>do not</u> boil. Remove from heat.
7. Garnish with pecans.

Serves 8

SALADS

Orange Sprinkle Salad

1 can (20 oz) crushed pineapple, drained

1 can (15 oz) mandarin oranges, drained

1 c coconut, shredded

1 carton small curd cottage cheese

1 (8 oz) Cool Whip

1 (3 oz) box orange Jell-O

Pecans

1. Mix pineapple, oranges, coconut and cottage cheese together.
2. Sprinkle Jell-O over fruit mixture and mix with a spatula.
3. Blend in Cool Whip; mix evenly.
4. Add a few pecans for accent.
5. Chill and serve.

Seven Layer Salad

Seven Layer Salad

iceberg lettuce, shredded

maple ham, cut in small cubes

celery, diced

onion, diced

carrots, shredded (optional)

frozen peas

4 eggs, hard boiled
and chopped

green and red bell peppers, diced

mayonnaise and sugar mixed to taste

sharp cheddar cheese, shredded

1. Layer ingredients in amounts desired.
2. Enjoy!

Patriotic Jell-O Salad

Patriotic Jell-O Salad

1 pkg (3 oz) each of cherry and blueberry Jell-O
1 ½ c water
1 c milk
1 envelope unflavored gelatin
¼ c cold water
1 c sour cream
½ c sugar
1 tsp vanilla

1. Soften gelatin in cold water.
2. Bring milk to a boil; add sugar and dissolve.
3. Add softened gelatin and cool slightly.
4. Add sour cream and vanilla; using an electric hand mixer, beat on low speed. Set aside to cool. (Be sure to keep mixture at room temperature).
5. In a separate bowl, dissolve blueberry Jell-O in 1 c boiling water; when dissolved add ½ c cold water.
6. Pour blueberry Jell-O carefully into a lightly oiled 7 X 11" glass dish; refrigerate until firm.
7. Carefully, not to disturb the blueberry layer, add cream mixture and refrigerate until firm.
8. In a separate bowl, dissolve cherry Jell-O in 1 c boiling water; when dissolved add ½ c cold water.
9. Carefully spoon warm cherry Jell-O on top of firm cream mixture and refrigerate 5-6 hours before serving.

Serves 12

Pretzel Salad

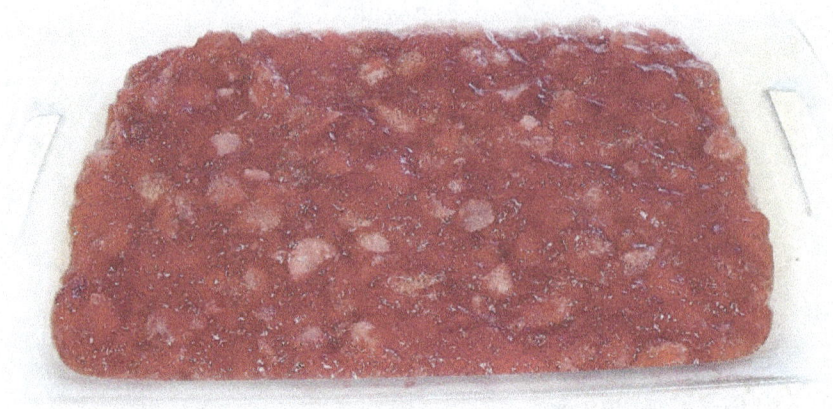

Crust
2 heaping cups pretzels, crushed
¾ c margarine, melted
1 T sugar

Filling
1 pkg (8 oz) cream cheese, softened
1 c sugar
1 (8 oz) Cool Whip

Top Layer
1 pkg (6 oz) strawberry Jell-O, regular
20 oz frozen strawberries
2 c boiling water

Crust
1. Mix together pretzels, margarine and sugar.
2. Pour into a 9 X 13" glass baking dish. Spread to cover bottom.
3. Bake at 400°F for 8 minutes. (Do not overbake.)
4. Cool to room temperature.

Pretzel Salad

Filling
1. In a small mixing bowl, add cream cheese and sugar. Mix well.
2. Fold in Cool Whip.
3. Spread on cold crust.

Top Layer
1. Dissolve strawberry Jell-O with boiling water.
2. Add frozen berries. Allow to set 10 minutes. Mix well.
3. Carefully pour on top of cream mixture.
4. Refrigerate until serving.

Serves 12-16

Cranberry-Pineapple Salad

1 pkg (6 oz) raspberry gelatin
1 ½ c boiling water
1 can (16 oz) jellied cranberry sauce
1 can (8 oz) crushed pineapple, undrained
¾ c orange juice
1 tsp lemon juice
½ c walnuts, chopped
lettuce leaves
mayonnaise

1. In a bowl, dissolve gelatin in boiling water.
2. Break up cranberry sauce and add to gelatin.
3. Add pineapple, orange juice and lemon juice. Chill until partially set.
4. Stir in nuts. Pour into a 7 X11" glass dish and chill until firm.
5. Cut into squares. Serve each on a lettuce leaf and top with mayonnaise.

Serves 12

Pineapple Chicken Salad Sandwiches

2 c chicken breasts, baked and cubed
½ c pineapple, crushed, drained
¼ c pecans, chopped
¼ c celery, chopped
2 T onion, finely chopped
2 T sweet pickle relish
½ c mayonnaise
¼ tsp onion salt
¼ tsp garlic salt
¼ tsp paprika
6 lettuce leaves
6 croissants

1. In a small bowl, combine chicken, pineapple, pecans, celery, onion, and relish.
2. Combine mayonnaise, onion salt, garlic salt and paprika. Add to chicken mixture and mix well.
3. Serve on lettuce-lined croissants.

Potato Salad

5 medium-large potatoes, peeled and cut
1 bunch large green onions, diced
3 stalks celery, diced
1 small carrot, diced
5 large eggs, boiled, cut up
¾ tsp salt
1 tsp dry mustard
3 T cider vinegar
2 T vegetable oil
paprika, salt to taste
curly parsley
¾ c mayonnaise to suit

1. Boil potatoes. Drain and set aside until cold.
2. Cut potatoes in small pieces; place in a large mixing bowl.
3. Boil eggs; place in ice cold water; peel and set aside.
4. Add diced onions, celery and carrots to the potatoes.
5. Sprinkle oil and vinegar over potatoes. Blend. Cover and let marinate in refrigerator for 4 hours.
6. Add eggs and mix.
7. Mix mayonnaise and dry mustard together; blend thoroughly with potato mixture.
8. Place in serving bowl; garnish with parsley and sprinkle paprika on top.

Sliced black olives and chopped pickles may also be added as desired.

Crab Pasta Salad

The medley of crab, pasta and vegetables in a creamy dressing makes this a special salad for company as well as every day.

2 c tricolor spiral pasta, uncooked
2 c imitation crabmeat, chopped
1 c (8 oz) sour cream
½ c mayonnaise
¾ tsp celery seed
¾ tsp garlic powder
¼ tsp salt
pepper to taste
1 c fresh broccoli florets
1 c fresh cauliflower (optional)

1. Cook and season pasta according to the package directions. Drain and rinse in cold water.
2. In a bowl, combine crab, sour cream, mayonnaise, celery seed, garlic powder, salt and pepper.
3. Stir in pasta, broccoli and cauliflower (optional).
4. Cover and refrigerate at least 2 hours before serving.

Serves 6-8

BREADS

Beverly's Chicken Croquettes

Filling
1 (15 oz) canned chicken, drained
1 pkg (8 oz) cream cheese, softened
1 heaping T onion, chopped
¼ tsp black pepper

Pastry
1 Pillsbury crescent seamless dough sheet

Filling
1. Combine chicken, cream cheese, onion and pepper. Mix well.
2. Refrigerate overnight.

Pastry
1. Unroll crescent dough and lay out on baking sheet. Cut into 8 squares.
2. Take one at a time and pat out.
3. Place a spoonful of chicken mixture on it; pull up the corners and sides together and twist.
4. Pat it down and place it on baking sheet.
5. Bake in pre-heated oven at 350°F for 15-17 minutes or until brown.

If desired, heat 1 can of Heinz Home Style Chicken Gravy and put over croquettes when serving. This is a quick and easy meal.

H.

Swedish Tea Ring

1 pkg active dry yeast
1 ½ c warm water (110-115°F)
¼ c sugar
¼ c Canola oil
2 egg whites, beaten
1 ¼ tsp salt
5 ½ to 6 c all-purpose flour, sifted
1 c walnuts, chopped
½ c maraschino cherries, patted dry, chopped
1/3 c brown sugar
1 tsp cinnamon
Pam non-stick spray
2 T butter, melted
candied cherries and pecans for garnish

<u>Icing</u>
1 c confectioner's sugar, sifted
1-2 T low-fat milk

Swedish Tea Ring

1. In a large mixing bowl, dissolve yeast in warm water.
2. Add sugar, oil, egg whites, salt and 1 c flour. Beat until smooth.
3. Stir in enough flour to form a soft dough.
4. Transfer to a floured surface and knead about 6 minutes until smooth.
5. Place in a bowl coated with non-stick cooking spray. Turn once to coat top. Cover and let rise for 1 hour or so.
6. Combine walnuts, cherries, brown sugar and cinnamon. Set aside.
7. Punch down dough; transfer to a lightly floured surface and roll out to a 12 X 18" rectangle.
8. Brush with butter; sprinkle with nut mixture to within ½" of edges.
9. Roll up tightly, jellyroll style, starting with the long side. Seal ends.
10. Place seam side down on a 14" pizza pan, sprayed. Pinch ends together to form a ring.
11. With scissors, cut from outside edge 2/3 of the way towards the center of the ring at 1" intervals.
12. Separate strips slightly so filling shows. Cover and let rise until doubled.
13. Bake at 375°F for 20-25 minutes or until golden brown. Cool.
14. Mix icing ingredients together until smooth.
15. Drizzle icing over ring and garnish with candied cherries and nuts.

Refrigerated Potato Rolls

2 large potatoes
1 ½ c warm potato water
2/3 c sugar
1 ½ tsp salt
1 pkg Fleishman's dry yeast
¼ c water, lukewarm
2 eggs, lightly beaten
2/3 c soft Crisco shortening
1 c mashed potatoes, lukewarm
7 c flour, sifted
Soft butter for glaze

Refrigerated Potato Rolls

1. Peel potatoes. In a saucepan add potatoes and water to cover. (Enough to make 1½ c potato water and 1 c mashed potatoes). Boil 20-30 minutes until potatoes are cooked.
2. Remove potatoes from water and mash.
3. Dissolve 1 envelope dry yeast in ¼ c water, lukewarm. Add yeast to 1 ¼ c warm potato water.
4. In a large mixing bowl, mix together, using dough hooks, 1 ¼ c potato water mixture, sugar and salt. Stir until blended.
5. Add eggs and soft Crisco shortening. Mix until blended.
6. Add warm mashed potatoes. Mix.
7. Gradually add flour. Mix until dough forms a soft ball.
8. Place dough on a lightly floured cloth or board and knead until smooth.

   (Dough hooks do much of the work. H.)

1. Place dough in a covered bowl and refrigerator overnight.
2. About 2 hours before baking, shape dough into desired rolls; place onto a greased 11 X 15" baking sheet. Cover and let rise 1 ½ -2 hrs.
3. Bake at 400°F for 12-15 minutes or until light brown.
4. Remove from oven and brush tops with butter.

Cheese Braid Coffee Cake

Dough
1 c sour cream
½ c sugar
¼ c butter and ¼ c margarine, melted
1 tsp salt
2 pkgs dry yeast
½ c warm water
2 eggs, beaten
4 ½ c flour

Filling
2 pkgs (8 oz) cream cheese, softened
¾ c sugar
2 egg yolks
1 tsp vanilla
dash salt

Glaze
2 c confectioner's suga
2-4 T milk
1 tsp vanilla
walnuts or pecans, finely chopped

This coffee cake freezes well when completely cooled and glaze has set. Wrap in paper towels and then foil. To thaw, remove foil only and let thaw at room temperature while still wrapped in towels.

Cheese Braid Coffee Cake

Dough

1. Heat sour cream on low. Stir in sugar, salt and butter/margarine mix. Cool to lukewarm.
2. In large bowl, soften yeast in water. Stir to dissolve.
3. Add sour cream mixture, eggs and flour. Mix well. Cover tightly and refrigerate overnight.
4. The next day divide dough into 4 equal parts. On a floured board, roll each part into an 8 X 12" rectangle.

Filling

1. In a small bowl combine cheese and sugar.
2. Add egg yolk, salt and vanilla. Mix well.
3. Spread ¼ of filling down the center of each rectangle to within 1 ½" of edge.
4. Using a sharp knife, cut dough at 1" intervals through margins and into small section of filling.
5. Overlap strips, one from each side, over filling on a slight angle to resemble a braid.
6. Transfer to a cookie sheet lined with parchment paper; cover and let rise until double in bulk, about 1 hr.
7. Bake at 350°F for 12-15 minutes.

Glaze

1. Combine sugar, milk and vanilla. Mix well.
2. Spread on warm braids.
3. Sprinkle with nuts.

Best Ever Banana Nut Bread

3 large <u>very ripe</u> bananas
¾ c sugar
1 egg
1 tsp baking soda

1 tsp baking powder
½ tsp salt
1 ½ c all-purpose flour
1/3 c butter, melted
½ c walnuts, chopped

1. Pre-heat oven to 375°F.
2. Using a mixer, mash bananas well.
3. Add sugar and egg. Mix well.
4. Add cooled melted butter. Mix.
5. Add soda, powder, salt and flour. Mix well.
6. Add chopped nuts to banana mixture. Mix but do not over beat.
7. Divide batter and place into 2 sprayed and floured 4X8" loaf pans.
8. Place in oven and bake approximately 35 minutes.
9. Remove from oven and immediately brush butter on top of loaves. Cool.
10. When cooled, remove from pans. Wrap in foil to store.

Freezes well.

Chocolate Zucchini Bread

1 ½ c vegetable oil
3 c sugar
4 eggs
1 tsp salt
3 oz unsweetened chocolate, melted
3 c fresh zucchini, grated
3 c all-purpose flour
½ tsp baking powder
1 ½ tsp baking soda
1 c walnuts, chopped

1. In a large mixing bowl, beat oil, sugar, eggs and salt until foamy.
2. Add chocolate and zucchini. Mix together.
3. In a separate bowl, mix together flour, powder and soda.
4. Add flour mixture and nuts to zucchini mixture. Mix well.
5. Bake at 375°F for 45-60 minutes. Test with a toothpick.
6. Remove from oven and brush with butter while hot. Cool in pans.
7. Remove from pans and finish cooling on wire racks.

Elegant Swan Lemon Cream Puffs

Batter
1 c water
½ c butter (no substitutes)
1 c all-purpose flour
4 eggs (room temperature)

Lemon Filling
2 eggs
2/3 c sugar
6 T lemon juice, freshly squeezed
4 T butter, cubed
1 c heavy whipping cream

Elegant Swan Lemon Cream Puffs

1. In a saucepan, bring water and butter to a boil.
2. Add flour all at once, stirring until it forms a smooth ball. Remove from heat and let stand 5 minutes.
3. Add eggs, one at a time, beating until mixture is smooth.
4. Drop by a large rounded spoonful, 3" apart, (enough dough for swan's body), onto a parchment-lined baking sheet.
5. Take ½ c dough; place in a pastry bag, using tip # 21 to make the head and neck for your swans.
6. Bake at 400°F for 30-35 minutes or until golden brown.
7. Remove to wire racks. Immediately remove the top 1/3 of each.
8. Discard soft dough from inside.
9. Set tops and bodies aside to cool.

1. For filling, in a heavy saucepan, combine the eggs, sugar, lemon juice, and butter.
2. Bring to a boil over medium heat; cook and stir for 5-7 minutes or until mixture is thick enough to coat a metal spoon.
3. Remove from heat. Cool quickly by placing pan in a bowl of ice water; stir for 3 minutes.
4. Transfer to a bowl and press plastic wrap onto surface of the filling. Chill 1 hour until partially set.
5. In a mixing bowl, beat cream and sugar until stiff peaks form. Fold into lemon mixture.
6. Fill cream puffs; place head and neck into front filling as shown.
7. Cut each top in 2 pieces for wings; place them on the sides.
8. Dust with confectioner's sugar.

Easy Waffles

2 c BISQUICK
1 egg
½ c oil
1-1/3 c Canada Dry Club Soda

1. In a bowl, mix all ingredients together. Blend well.
2. Pour in a hot waffle iron and cook until light brown or until light goes off.

Options: Add pecans or blueberries

Raisin Bran Muffins

5 c flour
3 c sugar
4 tsp baking powder
1 tsp salt
4 eggs
1 c vegetable oil
1 tsp vanilla
1 qt buttermilk
1 box (15 oz) Raisin Bran Cereal

1. Sift together flour, sugar, baking powder and salt. Set aside.
2. In large mixing bowl, beat together eggs, vegetable oil, vanilla, and buttermilk.
3. Add sifted ingredients.
4. Fold in Raisin Bran Cereal.
5. Transfer to lined muffin cups.
6. Bake at 400°F for 18-20 minutes or until a toothpick comes out clean.

Place excess batter in an air tight container and store in the refrigerator up to six weeks.
Simply delicious.
H.

Cinnamon Rolls

<u>Dough</u>
¾ c milk
½ c sugar
1 tsp salt
½ c margarine
½ c warm water
2 pkgs dry yeast
1 egg, beaten
4 c all-purpose flour

2 tsp butter
1/3 c brown sugar
1 tsp cinnamon
½ c pecans, chopped

<u>Glaze</u>
2 c confectioner's sugar
1 tsp vanilla
4-6 tsp milk (or more as needed)

Cinnamon Rolls

1. Scald milk. Stir in sugar, salt and margarine. Cool to lukewarm.
2. In a large bowl, add warm water. Sprinkle in ¼ tsp sugar and dry yeast. Stir to dissolve.
3. Stir in milk mixture, egg and ½ the flour. Beat until smooth.
4. Stir in remaining flour to make a stiff dough.
5. Cover tightly with foil and refrigerate several hours or overnight.
6. Punch down dough. Divide in half, cover and let rest for 10 minutes.
7. Line a 10½X16X2" baking sheet with parchment paper.
8. Roll each half into 12X18" rectangles. Spread with 2 T butter.
9. Sprinkle with brown sugar and cinnamon. Top with pecans.
10. Roll up jellyroll style beginning from the longest side.
11. Slice each half into 12 pieces.
12. Place cut side down in jellyroll pan. Cover and let rise until nearly double in size.
13. Bake at 350°F for 20-23 minutes or until nice and brown. Remove from oven and cool slightly.
14. Remove from pans onto a serving tray.
15. Drizzle with glaze.

<u>Glaze</u>
1. Add ingredients into a small mixing bowl. Beat well.

*Butter, brown sugar and cinnamon may be increased as desired. H.

CASSEROLES

Glenda's Amish Breakfast Casserole

1 lb. sliced bacon (sausage or ham may be substituted)
1 medium sweet onion
6 large eggs, slightly beaten (1-2 eggs more may be added for consistency as desired.)
4 c (1 bag) frozen shredded hash brown potatoes, thawed
2 c cheddar cheese, shredded
1 ½ c 4% cottage cheese
1 ¼ c swiss cheese, shredded (Gruyere or other flavorful cheese may be used)
salt and pepper to taste
optional additives: sautéed mushrooms and onions

1. Pre-heat oven to 350°F.
2. In a large skillet, cook bacon and onion until bacon is crisp; drain.
3. In a large bowl, combine remaining ingredients; add bacon mixture.
4. Transfer to a greased 9X13" baking dish. Top with additional cheese if desired.
5. Bake, uncovered, 35-40 minutes or until a knife inserted in the center comes out clean.
6. Let stand 10 minutes before cutting.

Serves 8

Baked Corn Casserole

Pam cooking spray
1 ½ sticks melted butter or margarine
1 can (15 oz) whole kernel corn, drained
1 can (15 oz) creamed corn (do not drain)
1 pkg Jiffy Corn Bread mix
3 T sour cream
2 eggs
2 T sugar
1 T pimentos

1. Lightly coat casserole dish with cooking spray.
2. Mix all ingredients together. Pour in the greased casserole dish.
3. Bake at 350°F for 40-60 minutes until center is solid.

Fourth of July Bean Casserole

½ lb. sliced bacon, diced
½ lb. ground beef
1 c chopped onion
1 can (28 oz) pork and beans
1 can (17 oz) lima beans, rinsed and drained
1 can (15-16 oz) kidney beans, rinsed and drained
½ c barbeque sauce
½ c catsup
½ c brown sugar
2 T prepared mustard
2 T molasses
1 tsp salt
½ tsp chili powder

1. In a large skillet, cook bacon, beef and onion until meat is brown and onion is tender. Drain.
2. Transfer to a greased 2 ½ qt baking dish.
3. Add all of the beans and mix well.
4. In a small bowl, combine remaining ingredients; stir into beef and bacon mixture.
5. Cover and bake at 350°F for 45 minutes. Uncover and bake another 15 minutes or more. (I bake longer. H.)

Yield: 12 servings

Spaghetti Pie

6 oz spaghetti
2 T butter
½ c Parmesan cheese
2 eggs, well beaten
1 lb. ground beef
½ c onion, chopped
¼ c green pepper, chopped
1 can (6 oz) tomato paste
1 tsp oregano, dried
¼ tsp garlic salt
4 tsp sugar
1 can (8 oz) tomato sauce
½ c Mozzarella cheese, shredded
1 c cottage cheese

Spaghetti Pie

<u>Crust</u>

1. Cook spaghetti as directed on the box. Drain.
2. Stir in butter, Parmesan cheese, and eggs.
3. Form mixture into a crust in a buttered 10" pie plate.

<u>Filling</u>

4. In a skillet, brown meat, onion and green pepper until vegetables are tender.
5. Stir in tomato paste, sauce, sugar, oregano and garlic salt. Heat through.

<u>Pie</u>

6. Spread cottage cheese over crust.
7. Fill pie with tomato mixture.
8. Bake at 350°F for 20 minutes.
9. Sprinkle with Mozzarella cheese and bake 5 minutes.

Serves 6-8.

Tossed salad and Italian bread go well with this dish.

H.

Reuben Crescent Bake

Reuben Crescent Bake

2 tubes <u>sheet</u> crescent rolls
1 lb. swiss cheese, sliced very thin
1 lb. Deli corned beef, sliced very thin
1 can (14oz) sauerkraut, rinsed and drained well
2/3 c Thousand Island dressing
1 egg white, slightly beaten
3 tsp caraway seeds

1. Unroll one tube of <u>sheet</u> crescent rolls. Press into one long rectangle.
2. Apply cooking spray to 9X13" glass baking dish. Press dough onto the bottom evenly.
3. Bake at 375°F for 8-10 minutes or until golden brown.
4. Over baked dough, layer half of the cheese and all of the Corned beef.
5. Combine sauerkraut and salad dressing.
6. Spread over beef; top with remaining cheese.
7. On a lightly floured surface, roll out the second tube of sheet crescent rolls. Place over cheese. Cut slits on top.
8. Brush with beaten egg white and sprinkle with caraway seeds.
9. Bake at 375°F for 25 minutes or until nicely browned. Let stand 5 minutes before serving.

Yield: 8 servings

Chicken Pot Pie

<u>Filling</u>
1 lb. fresh mushrooms, sliced
1 T butter
¼ c white wine (dry) or water
1 ½ c whipping cream
2 T flour
1 ½ tsp paprika
½ tsp salt
½ tsp black pepper
¾ c chicken broth
1 small bag of frozen peas and carrots
¼ c onion, diced
2 stalks celery, diced
1 small potato, diced
4+ c cooked chicken, cubed
1 egg

<u>Pie Pastry</u>
1 ½ c flour
1 tsp salt
1/3 c butter, chilled and cut into pieces
1 large egg
3-4 T ice water

Chicken Pot Pie

1. In a large saucepan, melt butter; add mushrooms and sauté until liquid is gone.
2. Add water (or wine), peas and carrots, onion, celery and potato; cook for 5 minutes on low-medium heat.
3. Blend flour, salt, pepper, and whipping cream until smooth.
4. Whisk into mushroom mixture.
5. Add chicken. Pour into a buttered 9X13" glass baking dish.
6. Cut up 2 T butter and apply to top of chicken mixture.

Top Crust Pastry
1. Stir flour and salt together; with a pastry blender; cut in butter.
2. Beat the egg and add into the water. Add egg mixture to flour mixture and blend to form a ball.
3. Roll out on a floured cloth or board. Cut into strips and place on top of pie for lattice look.
4. Bake at 350°F for 45-60 minutes until hot, bubbly and lightly browned.

Serves 8.

Steak Pot Pie

Filling
¼ c onion, chopped
¼ c sweet red pepper, chopped
¼ c green pepper, chopped
2 T Canola oil, divided
3 c boneless sirloin beef steak, ½" cubed
2 c frozen cubed hash brown potatoes
1 can (10oz) condensed cream of mushroom soup, undiluted
1 c baby carrots, sliced lengthwise
1 tsp Worcestershire Sauce
¼ c water
2 garlic cloves, minced
4 T butter, divided
½ c onions
1 c frozen green beans
1 c fresh mushrooms, sliced
¼ tsp salt
pepper to taste

1. In large skillet add 2 T butter, 1/4 c onion, 1 T oil and beef. Brown thoroughly.
2. Remove beef and season with pepper; keep warm.
3. In the same skillet, sauté remaining butter, 1 T oil, onions, mushrooms and garlic.
4. Add water. Stir in hash brown potatoes, carrots, green beans, red and green pepper, cream of mushroom soup, W. Sauce, salt and pepper. Bring to a boil.
5. Reduce heat; cover and simmer for 10-15 minutes.
6. Serve.

Steak Pot Pie

<u>Crust</u>
2 ½ c all-purpose flour
1 c butter-flavored shortening
4-5 T cold water
1 ¼ tsp salt
4 tsp onion, grated

1. Combine above ingredients, the same as making pie dough.
2. Divide dough in half. Roll out and place on the bottom and sides of a 10" glass pie dish.
3. Add filling.
4. Roll out second half of dough and place on top of pie. Seal and flute the edges. Cut slits.
5. Brush top with milk. Bake at 375°F for 1 hour or until bubbly and crust is browned.

Yield: 8 servings

Eggplant Casserole

Eggplant Casserole

2 medium eggplants
1 large sweet onion, thinly sliced
3 c V8 Juice
4 oz Mozzarella cheese, shredded
2 eggs, beaten
¾ c flour
basil, salt and pepper

1. Beat eggs in a bowl. Salt and pepper as desired. Set aside.
2. Wash and slice eggplants 1/3" thick; then remove the rind.
3. In a large heavy skillet, add oil or shortening to cover the bottom. Add heat.
4. In a shallow dish add flour, seasoned with salt.
5. Dip egg plant slices in egg and then flour mixture to cover. Brown both sides in heated skillet.
6. In a greased 9X9" baking dish, pour ¼ c V8 juice.
7. Layer eggplant, onion, cheese and V8 juice.
8. Top with cheese and bake at 350°F for 45 minutes or until browned.

Serves 4-5

Hash Brown Casserole

2 lb. frozen au gratin hash brown potatoes
1 ½ sticks margarine
1 can (10oz) cream of mushroom soup
1 tsp salt
¼ tsp pepper
½ c chopped onions
1 pt. sour cream
4 oz shredded sharp cheddar cheese
1 c diced ham
<u>Topping</u>
1 c corn flake crumbs
½ c melted butter
paprika
parsley

1. Defrost potatoes in melted margarine.
2. Add remaining ingredients to blend.
3. Put in a sprayed 9X13" glass baking dish.
4. Mix corn flakes and melted butter. Sprinkle over top of potatoes.
5. Shake parsley and paprika on top.
6. Bake at 350°F for 40 minutes.

Serves 8.

ENTREES

Citrus Sauce Pork Chops

1 can (14 oz) chicken broth
¼ c cornstarch, divided
6 (1/2" or 1") pork chops
salt and pepper
1 T corn oil
2 c orange juice
1 c baby carrots
2 T minced green onions
3 T honey
1 T white vinegar
2 T light corn syrup
1 T Dijon Mustard
2 T jellied cranberry sauce
2 tsp soy sauce
2 T fresh parsley, minced

Citrus Sauce Pork Chops

1. In a small bowl, stir together ¼ c chicken broth and 2 T corn starch until smooth. Set aside.
2. Season pork chops with salt and pepper; coat lightly with remaining 2 T cornstarch.
3. Heat oil in skillet on medium. Add pork chops.
4. Cook 10-15 minutes, turning once, until done. Remove from skillet and keep warm in oven.
5. Drain excess fat from skillet. Add remaining chicken broth, orange juice, onions and carrots. Simmer 15 minutes until carrots are done.
6. Stir honey, corn syrup, vinegar, mustard, cranberry sauce and soy sauce into corn starch mixture.
7. Add to skillet, stirring constantly. Bring to a boil over medium heat and boil 1 minute. Stir in parsley.
8. Return pork chops to skillet until heated through.
9. Serve with rice if desired.
10. Garnish with slices of fresh orange.

Pepperoni Spinach Quiche

Pepperoni Spinach Quiche

1 tube (8oz) crescent rolls
1 large red pepper, chopped
1 T olive oil
1 garlic clove, minced
5 eggs, lightly beaten
½ c Mozzarella cheese, shredded
½ c frozen chopped spinach, thawed and squeezed dry
¼ c sliced pepperoni, cut into strips
¼ c half & half cream
2 T Parmesan cheese, grated
1 T fresh parsley, minced
1 T fresh basil, minced or 1 tsp dried basil
dash pepper

1. Separate crescent dough into 8 triangles. Place in an ungreased 9" fluted tart pan with removable bottom, points to center.
2. Press onto bottom and up the sides to form a crust.
3. Seal seams and set aside.
4. In a small skillet, sauté red pepper in oil until tender. Add garlic and cook 1 minute longer. Remove from heat.
5. In another small bowl, combine the remaining ingredients.
6. Stir in red pepper mixture and pour onto crust.
7. Bake at 375°F for 25-30 minutes or until a knife inserted near the center comes out clean.
8. Let stand 5 minutes before cutting.

Yield: 8 servings

Garden Fresh Stromboli Rolls

2 ¾ c all-purpose flour, or as needed
1 T sugar
1 pkg rapid-rise yeast
2 T Hidden Valley Original Seasoning Mix
1 c water
1 T butter
8 slices each, swiss cheese, deli ham and sharp cheddar cheese, thinly sliced
½ c broccoli florets, lightly steamed
½ c banana peppers, thinly sliced
½ c zucchini, chopped
½ c green onions, thinly sliced
2 large plum tomatoes, thinly sliced
3 T Hidden Valley Seasoning Mix
¾ c cheddar cheese, shredded

I set out the cheeses and meats to take the chill off and make them easier to roll. H.

Garden Fresh Stromboli Rolls

1. In a large mixing bowl, blend 1 ½ c flour, sugar, yeast and seasoning mix.
2. In a saucepan, heat water and butter to 120-130°F.
3. Add butter mixture to dry ingredients until just moistened.
4. Stir in remaining flour to make a soft dough.
5. Turn onto a floured surface. Knead until smooth and elastic, 6-8 minutes.
6. Cover dough with a large bowl and let rest for 30 minutes.
7. Turn dough onto a lightly floured cloth or board. Roll into a 14X18" rectangle.
8. Place swiss cheese over the dough. Then layer ham, and cheese.
9. Top with broccoli, pepper, zucchini, onion and tomatoes.
10. Sprinkle seasoning mix over vegetables. Top with remaining shredded cheese.
12. Beginning at the long end, roll tightly; pinch the seam to seal. Place seam-side down. With a sharp knife cut the roll into 12 pieces.
13. Place cut-side down on a parchment lined 15X10X2" baking sheet.
14. Cover and let rise in a warm place until doubled in size (approximately 1 hour).
15. Bake at 400°F for 20-25 minutes or until lightly browned.

This recipe won first place at the Hidden Valley Cooking Contest in 2008 at the Canfield Fair, Canfield, Ohio.

H.

Baked Chicken Salad Wreath

2 pkgs crescent rolls
2 ½ c cooked chicken breasts (cubed)
½ c celery, finely chopped
¼ c onion, finely chopped
½ c mushrooms, finely chopped (sautéed in 2 T butter)
½ c dried cranberries, steamed

½ c Feta cheese
½ c walnuts (reserve 2 T to sprinkle on filling)
½ c + 2 T mayonnaise
1 tsp Dijon mustard
1 egg white, slightly beaten

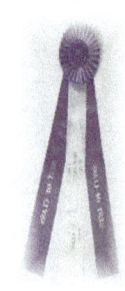

1. In a large mixing bowl, combine above ingredients.
2. Place crescent rolls on a large pizza stone or baking sheet to form a circle. Very carefully place short ends together and fold back each tip.
3. Place mixture down center of dough.
4. Sprinkle remaining walnuts on top. Overlap the crescent roll tips over each other to resemble a braid.
5. With a pastry brush. Apply egg whites to braid.
6. Place in oven and bake at 350°F for 40-45 minutes or until nicely browned.
7. Garnish with sprigs of parsley.

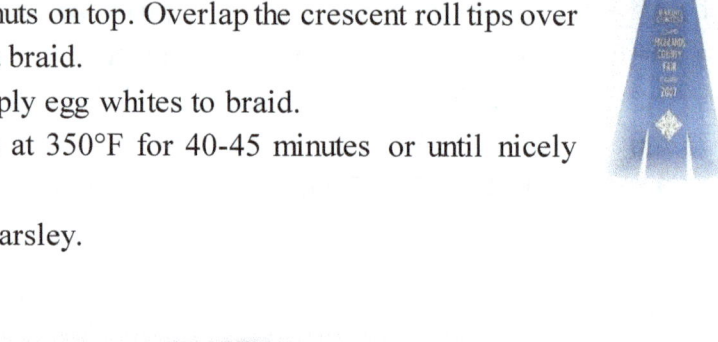

Ruthie's Meat Loaf

<u>Meat Loaf</u>
1 lb. ground beef
1 c milk
1 egg
¼ tsp pepper
1 c bread crumbs
2 T onions, chopped
1 tsp Worcestershire Sauce

<u>Topping</u>
½ c catsup
1 T mustard
3 T brown sugar
¼ tsp salt
½ c water

1. Mix meat loaf ingredients together in a large bowl.
2. In a baking pan, shape into a loaf.
3. Mix topping ingredients together and pour over loaf.
4. Bake covered at 350°F for 1 ¼ hours or until done.
5. Remove. Allow to set several minutes and serve.

DESSERTS

Philly Cream Cheese Frosting

1 pkg (8 oz) cream cheese, softened
4 T butter, softened
½ tsp vanilla
dash salt
5 c confectioner's sugar, sifted

Optional Ingredients

<u>For vanilla</u>: 1 ½ tsp lemon juice and 1 tsp grated lemon rind
<u>Chocolate</u>: ¼ c cocoa or 2 squares melted semi-sweet baking chocolate.

1. Combine cream cheese, butter, vanilla and salt. Beat until fluffy.
2. Add optional ingredients (above).
3. Gradually add confectioner's sugar in ¼ c increments while mixing.

Frosts two 9" cakes.

Carrot Cake

4 eggs
1-1/3 c vegetable oil
2 ¼ c sugar
2 ¼ c all-purpose flour
2 tsp baking powder
2 tsp baking soda
½ tsp salt
2 tsp cinnamon
½ tsp ground cloves
½ tsp ground nutmeg
3 ¼ c carrots, finely grated
1 c walnuts, chopped
1 c crushed pineapple, well drained
2 pkg (8oz) cream cheese, softened
1 ½ c white chocolate chips, melted
1 stick unsalted butter, softened
2 tsp lemon rind, grated
walnuts, chopped

Cake
1. Preheat oven to 350°F.
2. Line the bottom of two 9" round cakepans with waxed paper. Leave sides of pans dry; no cooking oil is needed.
3. In a large mixing bowl, add eggs and oil. Using an electric mixer, beat for 2 minutes on medium speed.
4. Add 1 c sugar and continue mixing for 2 minutes.
5. Add remaining sugar and mix 3-4 minutes.
6. Combine flour, baking powder, baking soda, salt cloves, cinnamon and nutmeg; add to egg mixture, beating on low speed for 1 minute until blended.

(continue on p.71)

Carrot Cake

7. Add carrots, pineapple and walnuts; mix until well blended.
8. Divide batter evenly into the 2 pans.
9. Bake 60 minutes or until toothpick inserted in the center comes out clean.
10. Cool to room temperature on wire racks.
11. Run a knife around edges of cakepans and remove cakes.
12. Wrap in plastic and refrigerate overnight.

Icing
1. To prepare icing, place cream cheese in a mixing bowl. Beat with a mixer on medium speed until smooth.
2. Add melted chocolate a little at a time. Continue to beat on medium speed.
3. Add butter, a little at a time. Scrape down sides of bowl. Add lemon rind and mix until uniform.

Decorating
1. Remove cakes from refrigerator and unwrap plastic. Ice the top of one layer. Repeat with the second cake. Ice top and sides.
2. Press chopped walnut on the sides.

Serves 18

Key Lime Cake

Cake

1 pkg Lemon Cake Mix
¾ c vegetable oil
5 eggs
1 pkg (3 oz) lime Jell-O
¾ c orange juice
8 T confectioner's sugar

Icing

1 pkg (8oz) cream cheese, softened
1 T vanilla
½ stick butter, softened
1 lb. box confectioner's sugar, sifted
1 c pecans, chopped (toasted for flavor)

Key Lime Cake

Cake
1. In a large mixing bowl, combine cake mix, oil, eggs and Jell-O. Beat on medium speed.
2. While beating, slowly add orange juice. Beat 2 minutes.
3. Transfer batter equally into three 8" round cakepans, bottoms lined with wax paper. Leave sides dry.
4. Bake at 325°F for 23-25 minutes or until done. Do not overbake.
5. Cool layers 5 minutes. Remove from pans and place cakes on wire rack to finish cooling. While still warm, prick tops with a fork.
6. Combine ½ cup lime juice and 8 T confectioner's sugar. Brush all juice onto cake layers.
7. Wrap in plastic and refrigerate overnight.

Icing
1. Beat together first four icing ingredients.
2. Place bottom layer on a plate, apply some icing and pecans. Do the same on the second layer.
3. Place third layer on top and frost top and sides.
4. Use remaining pecans to decorate cake.

Serves 14-16.

Hummingbird Cake

Cake
3 c all-purpose flour
2 c sugar
1 tsp salt
1 tsp baking soda
1 tsp cinnamon
3 eggs, slightly beaten
2 c ripe bananas, mashed
1 ½ c vegetable oil
8 oz crushed pineapple, unsweetened, with liquid
1 ½ tsp vanilla extract
1 c nuts, chopped

Icing
¼ c shortening
2 T butter, softened
1 tsp lemon peel, grated
¼ tsp salt
6 c confectioner's sugar, sifted
½ c pineapple juice, unsweetened
2 tsp half& half cream
walnuts, chopped (optional)

Hummingbird Cake

<u>Cake</u>

1. In a large mixing bowl, combine flour, sugar, salt, soda and cinnamon.
2. Add eggs, bananas, oil, pineapple, and vanilla. Beat until uniform.
3. Stir in walnuts.
4. Pour equally into three 9" greased, floured and wax paper lined round pans. Keep sides dry and ungreased.
5. Bake at 350°F for 25-30 minutes or until a toothpick comes out clean.
6. Cool 10 minutes. Remove cakes from pans and transfer to wire racks and cool completely.

<u>Frosting</u>

1. In a large bowl, beat shortening, butter, lemon peel and salt until fluffy.
2. Add confectioner's sugar, ¼ c at a time, alternating with pineapple juice.
3. Beat in cream.
4. Spread between layers and on top and sides of cake.
5. Sprinkle with walnuts if desired.

Makes 18 servings

Earthquake Cake

Pam non-sick spray
1 ½ c coconut, flaked
1 ½ c pecan pieces
1 German Chocolate Cake Mix
1 box (3oz) French Vanilla Instant Pudding
4 eggs, beaten
1 tsp vanilla
1/3 c oil
1 ¼ c water
1 pkg (8 oz) cream cheese, softened
1 stick margarine, melted
1 (1 lb.) box confectioner's sugar, sifted

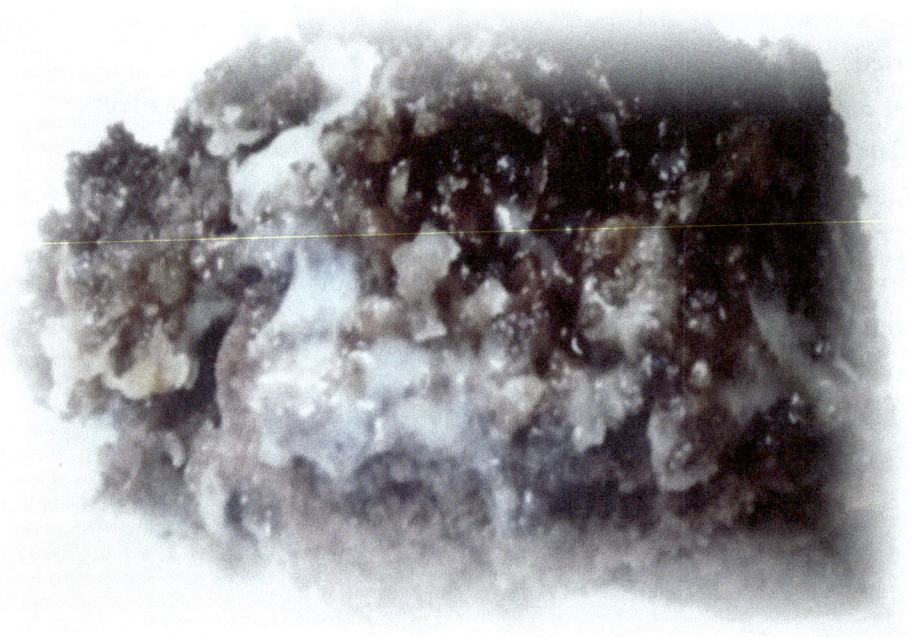

Earthquake Cake

1. Spray a 9X13" glass baking dish with cooking spray.
2. Spread one layer of coconut on bottom of dish.
3. Layer pecan pieces on the coconut.
4. In a large mixing bowl, blend together cake mix and instant pudding.
5. In a separate bowl, mix eggs, vanilla, oil and water. Then add egg mixture to dry cake mixture. Blend well.
6. Pour mixture over pecans and coconut.
7. Mix together cream cheese, margarine and confectioner's sugar. Pour over cake mixture.
8. Bake at 350°F for 50-55 minutes.

Simply Wonderful!

Woolworth's Icebox Cheesecake

Pam cooking spray
1 pkg (3oz) lemon Jell-O
1 c boiling water
1 pkg (8oz) cream cheese, softened
1 c sugar
1 can (8oz) crushed pineapple, drained
4 T fresh lemon juice
1 can (12oz) evaporated condensed milk, chilled
1 pkg (1 ¼ c) crushed graham crackers
2 T sugar
½ stick (4oz) butter, melted
1 can (8 oz) crushed pineapple, drained

Woolworth's Icebox Cheesecake

1. Dissolve Jell-O in boiling water. Cool until slightly thickened. (Set in a bowl of ice water to speed up thickening. Watch carefully.)
2. In a separate bowl, add crushed graham crackers, sugar and melted butter. Mix well.
3. Set aside 1/3 c graham cracker mix for top of finished cake.
4. Spray a 9X13" glass baking dish with cooking spray.
5. Put the remainder of cracker crumb mixture in a baking dish and bake at 400°F for 4 minutes. Set aside until cold.
6. In a large bowl, beat cream cheese and sugar until light.
7. Blend in drained crushed pineapple.
8. Add lemon juice and beat until smooth.
9. Gradually add Jell-O mixture and mix until smooth. Set aside.
10. In a separate bowl, beat evaporated milk until fluffy. Add cream cheese and Jell-O mixture and beat well.
11. Spread mixture over graham cracker crust.
12. Top with remaining crumbs. Chill well.

Serves 10-12.

This delicious recipe was given to me by my daughter, Glenda.
H.

Elegant Chocolate Torte

Batter
½ c butter, softened
1 ¼ c sugar
4 eggs, room temperature
1 tsp vanilla
1 ¼ c flour
1/3 c baking cocoa
¾ tsp baking soda
¼ tsp salt
1 ½ c chocolate syrup
½ c black liquid coffee (cold)

Filling
1/3 c all-purpose flour
3 T sugar
1 tsp salt
1 ¾ c milk
1 c chocolate syrup
1 egg (lightly beaten)
1 T butter
Frosting
2 c heavy whipping cream
¼ c chocolate syrup
¼ tsp vanilla

Elegant Chocolate Torte

Filling
1. In a small saucepan combine flour, sugar and salt.
2. Stir in milk and syrup until smooth.
3. Bring to a boil over medium heat, stirring constantly until smooth; cook and stir for 1-2 minutes until thickened. Remove from heat.
4. Stir a small amount of hot mixture into the egg; add egg mix to the hot mixture, stirring constantly.
5. Bring to a gentle boil; cook and stir for 2 minutes.
6. Remove from heat and add butter and vanilla.
7. Cool, stirring frequently.

Batter
1. In a large mixing bowl, cream butter and sugar until light and fluffy.
2. Add eggs, one at a time, mixing thoroughly after each addition.
3. Add vanilla.
4. In a separate bowl, combine flour, cocoa, soda and salt.
5. Add dry ingredients to the cream mixture alternating with syrup and coffee. Beat just until uniform.
6. Pour equally into two greased and floured 8" pans.
7. Bake at 350°F for 30-35 minutes. Test with a toothpick.
8. Cool for 10 minutes. Remove from pans and cool on wire racks.
9. Cut each layer in half horizontally.
10. Place one layer on a plate. Add 1/3 of the filling. Repeat layers twice more. Then top with remaining layer.

Frosting
1. In a mixing bowl, beat frosting ingredients until stiff; peaks form.
2. Spread over cake top and sides.
3. Garnish with chocolate curls and bits of Hershey's Chocolate Bars.

Linda's Chocolate Cake

2 c flour
2 c sugar
¾ c cocoa
2 tsp baking soda
1 tsp baking powder
1 tsp salt
2 large eggs, slightly beaten
¾ c evaporated milk
½ c corn oil
1 c hot coffee
1 tsp vanilla

1. Sift first 6 dry ingredients into a mixing bowl.
2. Add remaining ingredients. Mix to blend.
3. Pour batter equally into two greased and floured 9" pans or one 9X13" cake pan.
4. Bake at 300°F for 20-25 minutes or until a toothpick comes out dry.
5. When cool, frost with Linda's Chocolate Icing on p.83.
6. Slice and serve.

Linda's Chocolate Cake Icing

1 pkg (8 oz) cream cheese, softened
4 T butter, softened
1 tsp vanilla
1 T milk
3 T cocoa
5 ½ c confectioner's sugar, sifted

1. Combine softened cream cheese, butter, milk and vanilla, mixing until very fluffy and light.
2. Gradually add cocoa and then sugar, mixing well after each addition.
3. Frost cake.

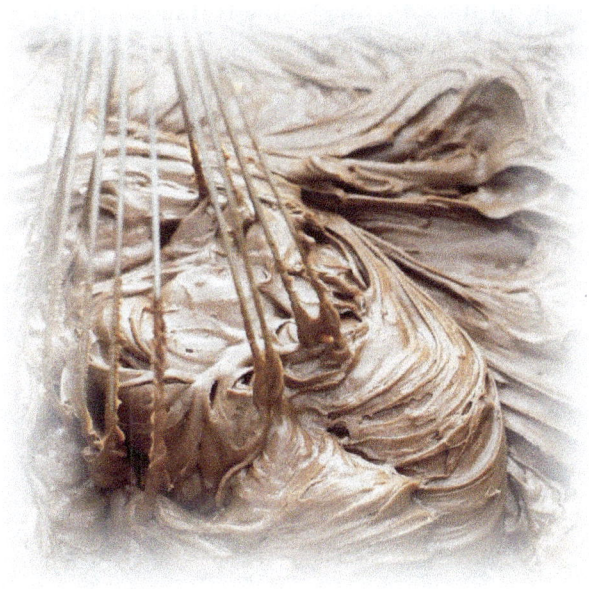

Strawberry Cookies

1 lb. coconut, finely ground

2 pkg (3 oz each) strawberry gelatin; reserve ½ pkg

¼ pound nuts, pecans or walnuts, ground

1 can (14 or 15 oz) sweetened condensed milk

4 T red sugar (may be made with red food coloring)

green Royal Icing or marzipan hulls

1. Mix ½ pkg reserved gelatin with red sugar. (add a drop or two of red food coloring to sugar to make red). Set aside.
2. Mix all ingredients (except reserved gelatin).
3. Take a small amount of mixture and shape it like a strawberry.
4. Roll each "strawberry" in the red gelatin/sugar mixture.
5. Add three small green Royal Icing leaves to the top of each berry. As an alternate, place a marzipan hull into the top of each. (See recipe for Royal Icing on p. 135.)

Strawberry Cookies

Amish Buttermilk Cookies

1 c shortening
1 c brown sugar
1 c white sugar
2 large eggs, room temperature
1 tsp vanilla
1 c buttermilk (<u>not</u> fat-free)
5 ¾ c flour
1 tsp baking soda
1 tsp baking powder
1 tsp salt
1 c raisins (steamed earlier)
3 or 3 ½ inch round cookie cutter

Amish Buttermilk Cookies

1. In a mixer, cream shortening and sugars. Beat until light and fluffy.
2. Add eggs and vanilla. Beat well.
3. Add drained steamed raisins.
4. Sift flour, baking soda, baking powder and salt together.
5. While mixing, add flour mixture, alternating with buttermilk.
6. Roll out dough on a floured board or cloth to not more than 3/8 inch thick.
7. Using a crinkled edge cookie cutter (shown below), cut out cookies and place on parchment lined baking sheets 2" apart.
8. Bake at 350° for 15-18 minutes or until very lightly browned.

Note: Check bottom of cookie for <u>no</u> brown color and touch top for doneness.

This was my Amish Gramma Yoder's recipe; it is one of my very favorite cookie recipes. Over the years I have made hundreds and hundreds of them.

H.

Deluxe Oatmeal Cookies

Deluxe Oatmeal Cookies

½ c plus 6 T butter, softened
¾ c brown sugar, firmly packed
½ c sugar
2 eggs, room temperature
1 tsp vanilla
1 ½ c all-purpose flour
1 tsp baking soda

1 tsp cinnamon
½ tsp salt (optional)
3 c Quaker Oats, quick or old-fashioned
1 c raisins, steamed, drained and cold or
1 c dried cranberries
1 c walnuts, chopped
1 c shredded coconut

1. Heat oven to 350° F.
2. Using an electric mixer, in a large bowl, beat butter and sugars on medium speed until creamy.
3. Add eggs and vanilla. Beat well.
4. In a separate bowl, sift together flour, baking soda, cinnamon and salt. Mix well.
5. Add oats, raisins, coconut and walnuts. Mix well.
6. Using a large cookie scoop, drop onto parchment lined baking sheets.
7. Bake 12-15 minutes or until lightly brown.
8. Let cool for 2 minutes, then remove from sheet and place on cooling rack.

Makes 30-32 cookies

Gingerbread Men Cookies

I remember making these cookies as a newlywed over 60 years ago. Over the years I have made many hundreds of these cookies and have shared them with family and friends over the Christmas holidays. H.

1/3 c soft shortening
1 c brown sugar, packed
1 ½ c (12oz) molasses
½ c cold water
6 c flour, sifted
1 tsp salt
1 tsp allspic
1 tsp ginger
1 tsp cloves

1 tsp cinnamon
2 tsp baking soda
3 T water
Steamed raisins for eyes and buttons
Sliced maraschino cherries for mouth
Royal Icing (optional) p. 135

Gingerbread Men Cookies

1. Preheat oven at 350° F.
2. Using an electric mixer, in a large bowl, cream shortening and sugar.
3. Gradually beat in molasses until well blended.
4. Pour water into empty molasses jar to rinse. Pour into batter.
5. In a separate bowl, sift together flour, salt, allspice, cloves, ginger and cinnamon.
6. Gradually add half the dry mixture to batter and mix completely.
7. Dissolve baking soda in 3 T water. Add to batter.
8. Finish adding dry ingredients. Mix until well blended.
9. Chill dough an hour or overnight.
10. On a floured cloth or board, roll out dough to about ½".
11. Using a gingerbread cookie cutter, cut cookies out of the dough and place cookie on a parchment lined baking sheet.
12. Place raisins for eyes and buttons and cherry slice for a mouth.
13. Place in preheated oven at 350°F and bake for 15-18 minutes or until no finger imprint remains when touched.
14. Cool for 2 minutes, then transfer to cooling racks.
15. Decorate with icing when cool. (optional)
16. When cool and decorated, wrap to avoid drying out.

This recipe may also be used to make Gingerbread Houses.

Butter Horns

Butter Horns

Dough
2 c flour
½ pound margarine, softened
1 egg yolk ¾ c sour cream

Filling
¾ c sugar
1 tsp cinnamon
1 c nuts, finely chopped

1. Preheat oven to 375° F.
2. Using an electric mixer, in a large bowl, cream flour and margarine together.
3. Add egg and sour cream. Mix well.
4. Shape dough into a ball. Chill for several hours.
5. In a separate bowl, combine sugar, cinnamon and nuts.
6. Separate chilled dough into four parts.
7. On a lightly floured cloth or board, roll each part into a circle 1/8 inch thick.
8. Sprinkle with ¼ nut mixture.
9. Cut into wedges.
10. Roll each wedge from the outside to the center.
11. Place on parchment lined baking sheet.
12. Repeat with the remaining three parts.
13. Bake 15-16 minutes until lightly browned.

Yield: 48-60 cookies

Pecan Tarts

<u>Dough</u>
4 sticks (1 lb.) margarine or butter (room temperature)
2 (8oz) cream cheese (room temperature)
4 c flour

<u>Filling</u>
1 c pecans (meal or pieces)
1 c dark corn syrup
1/8 tsp salt
3 eggs, beaten
1/3 c sugar
¼ c butter, melted

Pecan Tarts

Dough

1. Blend butter and cream cheese.
1. Add flour and mix well.
2. Refrigerate overnight. (Refrigerate until all dough is used.)

Filling

1. In a bowl, add eggs, sugar, salt, butter and corn syrup. Blend well.
2. Add nuts and mix.

Note: It will take four batches of filling for a full batch of dough.

Tart

1. Roll dough into 1" balls and using your thumb or a tart press, press into tart cups, leaving room for filling.
2. Spoon in filling. Stir each time before filling a tart to keep the filling well mixed and uniform.
3. Bake at 375°F for 15-18 minutes or until lightly brown. Let cool in tart pans.
4. Serve.

Makes 144 tarts

Peppermint Patty Sandwich Cookie

2 regular size devil's food cake mixes
4 eggs
2/3 cup canola oil
½ c granulated sugar
1 pkg (8oz) cream cheese, softened
½ c butter, softened
1 tsp peppermint extract
4 c confectioner's sugar, sifted

Peppermint Patty Sandwich Cookie

1. Preheat oven to 350°F.
2. In a large bowl, combine cake mixes, eggs, and oil. Beat until well blended.
3. Shape into 1" balls. Place 2" apart on greased baking sheets and flatten with bottom of a glass dipped in granulated sugar.
4. Bake 7-9 minutes or until tops are cracked. Cool 2 minutes before removing to wire racks to cool completely.
5. In a large bowl, beat cream cheese, butter and extract until blended. Gradually beat in confectioner's sugar until smooth.
6. Spread filling on bottoms of half the cookies.
7. Cover with the remaining cookies. (Refrigerate leftovers in an airtight container.

Sugar Cookies

Dough

4 ½ c flour, sifted
4 tsp baking powder
1 tsp salt
2 sticks unsalted butter, softened
2 c sugar
2 eggs
½ c milk
1 tsp vanilla

Icing

3 c confectioner's sugar, sifted
1/3 tsp Meringue Powder
5-6 T warm water, to make icing easier to brush

Dough

1. Preheat oven to 375°F.
2. Sift together flour, baking powder and salt.
3. Using an electric mixer, cream butter and sugar until fluffy.
4. Add eggs and beat well.
5. Add the dry ingredients, one cup at a time, alternating with milk and vanilla. Beat well after each addition.
6. Wrap and chill dough for at least one hour.
7. Divide dough into four pieces.
8. Roll one piece at a time on a lightly floured cloth or board until 1/3 inch thick.
9. Cut with cookie cutters into shapes desired.
10. Bake for 10-12 minutes. Cool on racks.
11. Decorate.

Sugar Cookies

<u>Icing</u>

1. Mix ingredients together.

<u>Cookie</u>

1. While the cookie is a bit warm, using a pastry brush, paint on icing to the edges. (It will flow nicely and hold.) Decorate one color at a time and dry between colors.
2. Let cookie get cold before storing.

Makes forty 3" cookies

This recipe has been proven by daughter Glenda to be
the best recipe for "Cut-outs". H.

Clothespin Cookies

1 pkg (2 sheets) Puff Pastry Sheets
½ c shortening
½ c margarine
1 c sugar
1 egg white
2 tsp vanilla
½ c hot milk
4" tapered pastry forms

Clothespin Cookies

1. Set one sheet Puff Pastry out at a time to thaw 20-25 minutes.
2. Pre-heat oven to 350°F.
3. On a lightly floured surface, roll out the thawed pastry to a 10X14" rectangle.
4. Using a pizza cutter, cut dough into ½ by 6" strips. Wrap each strip around a baking rod or dowel. Moisten slightly and seal the overlapping edges. Place on a parchment lined baking sheet.
5. Bake at 350°F for 11-13 minutes.
6. Carefully remove from rod or dowel and cool completely.
7. With an electric mixer on medium-high speed, beat together shortening and margarine. Gradually add 1 c sugar, beating well. Add egg white and vanilla. Beat thoroughly until fluffy and light. Add hot milk, 1 T at a time, beating until creamy. Chill an hour or more.
8. Using a pastry bag and #21 tip, pipe filling into each end of cooled cookie.
9. Lightly sift powdered sugar on filled cookies.
10. Repeat steps 3-9 with second pastry sheet.
11. Store in refrigerator in an air tight container. May be frozen.

Pastry Rods

Buckeyes

1 stick (¼ lb.) butter, softened
1 ½ c peanut butter
1 box (1 lb.) confectioner's sugar, sifted
1 tsp vanilla
2 bags chocolate melting chips
¼ c paraffin wax, shaved, unpacked

1. Combine butters: add vanilla and blend well.
2. Gradually add confectioner's sugar in ¼ c increments.
3. Form dough into 1" balls. Place in covered container.
4. Refrigerate overnight.
5. In a melting pot, add chocolate and paraffin. Mix thoroughly.
6. Holding ball on a toothpick, dip into melted chocolate.
7. Set out to dry on wax paper.

Buckeyes

In 2003, the state of Ohio celebrated it's Bicentennial. Our local County Fair commemorated this milestone anniversary with a craft competition featuring the Ohio State Nut, which is the Buckeye.

My husband served in the U.S. Navy; this inspired me to create a doll for each branch of the Military: Army, Navy, Air Force, Marines and Coast Guard, using the buckeye for each head

.I won a blue ribbon for this competition. H.

Triple Nut Diamond Cookies

1 c. allpurpose flour
½ c sugar
½ c cold butter, divided (no substitutes)
½ c brown sugar, packed
2 T honey
¼ c whipping cream
2/3 c each pecans, walnuts and almonds, chopped

Triple Nut Diamond Cookies

1. Line a greased 9" square glass baking dish with foil; grease the foil and set aside.
2. In a bowl, combine flour and sugar.
3. Cut in ¼ c butter until mixture resembles coarse crumbs.
4. Press into prepared baking dish.
5. Bake at 350°F for 10 minutes.
6. In a saucepan, heat brown sugar, honey and remaining butter until bubbly.
7. Boil 1 minute. Remove from heat.
8. Stir in cream and nuts.
9. Pour over crust and bake at 350°F for 16-20 minutes or until surface is bubbly.
10. Cool on a wire rack.
11. Refrigerate for 30 minutes.
12. Using foil, lift bars out of dish; cut into 1 ½ inch diamonds.
13. Store in air-tight container.

Makes approximately 3 dozen bars.

Apple Crisp

7 c baking apples, peeled and sliced
¾ c sugar
2 T flour
1/8 tsp salt
1 tsp cinnamon
¼ tsp nutmeg

Topping
1 c oatmeal
1 c brown sugar
¾ c flour
1 stick (¼ lb.) margarine or butter
¼ tsp baking soda
¼ tsp baking powder

1. Blend apples, sugar, salt, cinnamon and nutmeg. Pour into a 9X13" glass baking dish.
2. Using a blender, blend topping ingredients until crumbly. Scatter on top of apple mixture.
3. Bake at 375°F for 35-40 minutes or until bubbles form.

Serves 10-12.

Bread Pudding

4 eggs, beaten
½ c sugar
pinch of salt
1 c half & half
½ c milk
1/3 tsp nutmeg, fresh grated
1 tsp vanilla
¾ c raisins, steamed
6 slices butter-type white bread,
1" cubed
2 T butter, diced

1. In a mixing bowl, beat together eggs, sugar, salt, half & half, milk, nutmeg and vanilla.
2. Add raisins and then bread. Mix.
3. Pour into a 1 ½ quart buttered baking dish. Dot with butter and sprinkle nutmeg on top.
4. Bake at 350°F for 40 minutes or until lightly brown.

Serves 8-10

Amish Brown Sugar Dumplings

Amish Brown Sugar Dumplings

1 c brown sugar
1 T butter
¾ c milk, 4%
1 tsp vanilla
2 c flour
1½ tsp baking powder
¼ tsp salt
1 c walnuts, chopped

Syrup
2 ½ c brown sugar
2 ¼ c water
3 T butter
1 tsp vanilla

1. In a mixing bowl, add brown sugar, vanilla and butter; beat well.
2. Sift together flour, baking powder and salt. Add to sugar mixture, alternately with milk. Add walnuts and set aside.
3. Butter a 9X13" glass baking dish.

Syrup
1. In saucepan, heat together sugar, water, butter and vanilla until mixture comes to a boil.
2. Pour into a greased 9X13" glass baking dish.

Pudding
1. Take prepared batter and, using a large spoon, drop into the hot boiling syrup. (This is key!)
2. Bake at 325°F for 22-25 minutes or until lightly browned.
3. Let sit until cold. Serve.

This recipe is from my Gramma Yoder. H.

Amish Date-Nut Pudding

1 c dates, chopped
1 tsp baking soda
1 c boiling water
1 c sugar
1/3 c butter
1 large egg

½ tsp vanilla
1 ½ c flour
1 tsp salt
¾ c walnuts, chopped
1 pt. heavy whipping cream
1 tsp vanilla
4 T sugar

1. Place dates in bowl.
2. Sprinkle baking soda over dates.
3. Add boiling water over dates.
4. Set aside overnight to marinate.

Amish Date-Nut Pudding

Cake
1. In a mixing bowl, add sugar and butter. Beat well.
2. Add egg. Beat well.
3. Add date mixture. Mix well.
4. Add vanilla; continue mixing.
5. Add salt to flour; then add to above mixture. Mix well.
6. Blend in chopped nuts and pour into a greased and floured 9X9" glass baking dish.
7. Bake at 350°F for approximately 30 minutes. Do not overbake.
8. Let cake cool in baking dish.

Whipped Cream
1. Chill bowl and beaters first.
2. Whip whipping cream.
3. While beating, add 1 tsp vanilla and 4 T sugar.

Pudding
1. Cut cake into 1 ½ - 2" pieces and place into serving bowl a few pieces at a time.
2. Add some whipped cream and blend. Repeat until all cake and cream is used.

This was one of my Gramma Yoder's favorite desserts. It is very moist and delicious.
H.

Vanilla Pudding

Vanilla Pudding

2/3 c sugar
½ tsp salt
2 ½ T cornstarch
1 T flour
3 c milk
3 egg yolks, slightly beaten
1 T butter
1 ½ tsp vanilla
Bananas (optional)
Graham crackers, crushed (optional)

1. In a sauce pan, mix together sugar, salt, cornstarch and flour.
2. Gradually stir in milk. Cook over medium heat, stirring constantly, until mixture thickens and boils.
3. Lightly boil one minute; remove from heat.
4. Slowly add 1/3 of the mixture into egg yolks.
5. Add egg mixture back into saucepan. Boil 1 minute, stirring constantly. Remove from heat.
6. Blend in butter and vanilla. Cool.
7. Add banana slices and graham cracker crumbs as desired.
8. Top with graham cracker crumbs or whipped cream as desired.

Butter Pie Crust

1 ½ c all-purpose flour
1 tsp salt
1 tsp sugar
1 c cold butter
¼ c cold water
1 scant tsp cider vinegar

1. Using a food processor, combine flour, salt, and sugar.
2. Add butter until mixture resembles coarse crumbs.
3. Gradually add water until dough is soft ball consistency.
4. Cover and refrigerate 1 hour or until easy to handle.

Makes two 9" crusts

Classic Crisco Pie Crust

2 c all-purpose flour
1 tsp salt
¾ stick Crisco (butter-flavored) shortening, well chilled
1 tsp cider vinegar
4 to 8 T water, ice cold

1. Using a food processor, blend flour and salt.
2. Cut in shortening until coarse crumbs form.
3. Blend in cider vinegar and enough water just until dough holds together.
4. Divide dough in half. Shape into ½" thick discs. Wrap each disk in plastic wrap. Chill 15 minutes.
5. On a lightly floured surface, roll out each disc 2" larger than a 9" pie dish.
6. Place disc into the pie dish.
7. Bake at 375°F for 10 minutes or until lightly brown or continue to make pie with unbaked crust as the pie recipe calls for.

Note: Always have oven up to temperature and know whether to pre-bake the crust before filling.

Strawberry Rhubarb Pie

unbaked crusts for a two-crust pie
1 ½ c sugar
6 T flour

¼ tsp cinnamon
3 c rhubarb, cut up
3 c fresh strawberries, sliced
1 ½ T butter

1. In a large mixing bowl, blend together sugar, flour and cinnamon.
2. Add rhubarb and strawberries; blend slightly.
3. Pour filling into a pastry-lined 9" pie dish; dot with butter.
4. Cover with top crust; seal and flute edges of crust and sprinkle with sugar. Cut slits in the top crust. (A lattice top-crust is optional.)
5. Bake at 425°F for 15 minutes. Reduce temperature to 375°F and bake another 25-30 minutes or until crust is nicely browned and juice begins to bubble through the slits.
6. Serve warm.

Libby Pumpkin Pie

1 ½ c sugar	4 large eggs
1 tsp salt	1 can (29oz) pumpkin
2 tsp cinnamon	2 cans (12oz) Carnation evaporated milk
1 tsp ginger	2 unbaked pie shells, 9"
½ tsp cloves	

1. In a small bowl, mix sugar, salt, cinnamon, cloves and ginger.
2. In a large mixing bowl, lightly beat eggs.
3. Stir in pumpkin and the sugar mixture. Gradually add in evaporated milk.
4. Pour into unbaked pie shells.
5. Bake at 425°F for 15 minutes. (Add a "Crust Cover" to prevent crust from burning.)
6. Reduce temperature to 350°F and bake 40-50 minutes or until knife inserted in the center comes out clean.

Makes 2 pies

Use any remaining dough to cut out small leaves; bake in oven for 7-8 minutes. Place on pie about 20 minutes before pie is done. H.

Apple Dumplings

Syrup Glaze
2 c water
1 c sugar
2 T Red Hots

Apples
4 large baking apples, room temperature
2 T fresh lemon juice

Dumpling Dough
1-1/3 cups all-purpose flour
¼ tsp salt
6 T (2/3 c) butter-flavored Crisco
4 T water (if needed)

Apple Preparation
1 c sugar
1 tsp cinnamon
1/8 tsp ground allspice
2 T all-purpose flour

Make glaze before preparing apples or dough. It saves time.

Glaze
1. In a saucepan add water, sugar and Red Hots. Bring to a boil.
2. Turn down heat to medium and cook down until syrupy for glaze.

Apples
1. Peel and core apples.
2. Place in water with lemon juice. (to prevent browning) Set aside.

Note: Apples can be sliced if preferred.

Apple Dumplings

Dough
1. In large mixing bowl, sift together flour and salt.
2. With pastry blender add Crisco.
3. Gradually add water as needed to make a soft ball of dough.
4. Shape into 4 balls. Cover to keep moist.
5. Roll out each ball. Trim out 4 corners to reduce too much pastry around apple.

Seasoning Mixture
1. Mix sugar, cinnamon, allspice and flour.
2. Roll each apple into mixture.

1. Pre-heat oven to 400°F.
2. Place seasoned apple in each dough circle.
3. Put 1 T seasoning in core.
4. Add 1 tsp butter to core.
5. Wrap apples with dough. Take cut-off pieces of dough and place on apple top to form leaves.
6. Bake for 15 minutes. Reduce temperature to 375°F and bake for another 35 minutes or until nicely browned.
7. Every 15 minutes baste glaze over apples.
8. Serve.

Fresh Black Raspberry Pie

<u>Filling</u>
5 c black raspberries
1-1/3 c sugar
2 T tapioca
2 T cornstarch
½ tsp cinnamon

<u>Dough</u>
2 c all-purpose flour
1 T sugar
1 tsp salt
¾ c butter-flavored shortening
6 T water (to form a soft ball)
1 tsp cider vinegar
1 T butter
1 T milk
1 T sugar

Fresh Black Raspberry Pie

1. Combine raspberries, sugar, tapioca and cornstarch. Let stand 15 minutes.

Dough
1. Mix together flour, sugar, salt and shortening until small crumbles form.
2. Add vinegar and water; mix with a fork.
3. Using hands, form 2 balls and flatten.
4. Wrap in plastic wrap and refrigerate for 20 minutes.
5. Place on a lightly floured cloth or board. Roll out one ball to form a circle. Place in a 9" pie dish.
6. Add raspberry mixture; dot with butter.
7. Roll out a second ball to form a circle. Cut designs or strips to form a lattice topping. Seal and flute edges.
8. Mix milk and sugar and brush on top.
9. Bake in pre-heated oven at 375°F for 20 minutes; turn temperature down to 350°F and bake for another 25-30 minutes or until bubbly.

Yield: 8 servings

Washington State Apple Pie

Washington State Apple Pie

7 c baking apples, sliced
2 T water
1 T lemon juice
½ c sugar
½ c brown sugar, packed
3 T flour

1 tsp cinnamon
¼ tsp nutmeg
1/8 tsp ginger
1/8 tsp salt
unbaked pastry for a 2-crust pie
4 tsp butter

1. In a saucepan combine apples, water, and lemon juice. Cook covered over low-medium heat until apples are tender, not mushy. Remove from heat. <u>Do not</u> drain.
2. In a large bowl, combine sugar, flour, cinnamon, nutmeg, ginger and salt. Pour over the apples and toss to coat.
3. Place bottom pastry in pie dish. Add apple mixture.
4. Dot with 4 tsp butter. Cover with top pastry. Seal and flute edges. Cut slits in top crust.
5. Bake at 450°F for 10 minutes. Reduce heat to 350°F and bake for 35-45 minutes longer or until golden brown.

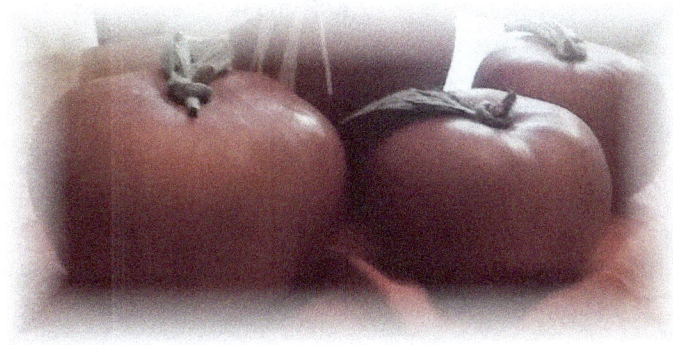

Meringue

3 egg whites, room temperature
¼ tsp cream of tartar
6 T sugar
½ tsp vanilla (optional)
½ tsp lemon juice (optional)

1. Beat egg whites and cream of tartar until forming peaks.
2. Gradually add sugar. Beat until stiff.
3. Add vanilla for butterscotch pie or lemon juice for lemon meringue pie.

Butterscotch Pie

9" baked pie crust
6 T butter
1 c dark brown sugar
1 c boiling water
3 T cornstarch
2 T flour
½ tsp salt
1-2/3 c milk
3 egg yolks, slightly beaten
1 tsp vanilla

1. In a large heavy skillet, over low heat, melt butter until golden brown.
2. Add brown sugar. Boil until foamy (2-3 minutes), stirring constantly.
3. Stir in boiling water. Remove from heat.
4. In a separate bowl, gradually combine cornstarch, flour, salt and milk. Mix until smooth.
5. Add milk mixture to skillet, stirring constantly. Over low heat, bring to a boil. Remove from heat.
6. Stir 1/3 of above mixture into slightly beaten egg yolks.
7. Stir the egg yolk mixture into the skillet mixture. Boil 1 minute. Remove from heat.
8. Blend in vanilla. Pour into a 9" pie shell.
9. Cover pie with meringue.
10. Bake at 375°F for 10-12 minutes or delicately brown.

Lemon Meringue Pie

9" baked pie crust
1 ½ c sugar
1/3 c cornstarch
1 ½ c water

3 egg yolks, slightly beaten
3 T butter
4 T lemon juice
1-1/3 T lemon zest

1. In a saucepan combine sugar and cornstarch; gradually whisk in water. Whisk until smooth with no lumps.
2. Cook over moderate heat, stirring constantly until mixture thickens and comes to a boil. Boil 1 minute.
3. Slowly add 1/3 of above mixture into beaten egg yolks. Mix.
4. Stir egg mixture into the hot mixture in saucepan. Boil 1 minute longer, stirring constantly until smooth.
5. Blend in butter, lemon juice, and lemon zest.
6. Pour into baked pie shell.
7. Top with meringue.
8. Bake at 375°F for 10-12 minutes or until delicately brown.

MISCELLANEOUS

Veggie Pizza

2 pkgs crescent rolls
1 pkg (8 oz) cream cheese, softened
1 c mayonnaise
3 T onions, grated
2 carrots, shredded
1 c broccoli, small pieces
1 c cauliflower, small pieces
½ c red pepper, diced

1. Place crescent roll dough on a baking sheet to form a round pizza-type crust. Seal edges and using a fork, poke small holes in dough to minimize bubbling,
2. Bake as directed on dough package or until golden brown. Cool.
3. Mix cream cheese, mayonnaise and onions until creamy.
4. Spread cream cheese mixture on cooled dough.
5. Top with veggies and refrigerate.
6. Serve cold.

Club Roll-Ups

1 pkg (8 oz) cream cheese, softened
½ c ranch dressing
2 T ranch dressing mix
8 bacon strips, baked and crumbled
½ c green onions, finely chopped
1 can (2 ½oz) ripe olives, sliced
½ c green olives, sliced
1 small jar pimentos, diced
½ c canned jalapeno peppers, diced
½ head iceberg lettuce, sliced thinly
4oz + sharp cheddar cheese, shredded
8 (10") flour tortillas

1. In a small mixing bowl, beat cream cheese, ranch dressing and dressing mix until well blended.
2. In another bowl, combine bacon, onion, olives, pimentos and jalapenos.
3. Spread cheese mixture over tortillas; follow with bacon mixture.
4. Sprinkle with lettuce and cheese mixture. Roll up.
5. Wrap in wax paper; place in sealed container and refrigerate.
6. Cut the ends off for better appearance before serving.
7. Cut in slices, halves or thirds and serve.

Use 8 slices thin sliced deli ham, roast beef or turkey and omit lettuce as desired. They are good either way.

Fruit Pizza

1 c all-purpose flour
¼ c confectioner's sugar
½ c cold butter
1 pkg (8oz) reduced-fat cream cheese, softened
1/3 c sugar
1 tsp vanilla
2 c fresh strawberries, halved
1 can (11oz) mandarin oranges, drained well
1 c fresh blueberries
1 can (8oz) pineapple tidbits, drained
3 Kiwi, thinly sliced

<u>Glaze</u>
4 tsp corn starch
1 ¼ c pineapple juice
1 tsp lemon juice

Fruit Pizza

Pizza

1. In a large bowl, combine flour and confectioner's sugar.
2. Cut in butter until crumbly.
3. Press into a 12" circle on a ceramic pizza stone or ungreased pizza pan.
4. Bake at 350°F for 10-12 minutes or until lightly browned. Cool on a wire rack.
5. In a small mixing bowl, beat cream cheese, sugar and vanilla until smooth. Spread over cooled crust.
6. Arrange strawberries, oranges, pineapple, Kiwi and blueberries on top.

Glaze

1. In a small saucepan, combine cornstarch, pineapple juice and lemon juice until smooth.
2. Bring to a boil; cook and stir for 2 minutes or until thickened.
3. Cool slightly. Drizzle over fruit.
4. Refrigerate until chilled.
5. Slice and serve as an appetizer, entrée or dessert.

Caramel Corn

9 qt popped popcorn (remove un-popped kernels)
½ c Karo Light Syrup
2 c brown sugar
1 c margarine or butter
½ tsp baking soda
2 T vanilla

1. In a saucepan, add Karo syrup, sugar and butter. Boil 5 minutes. Remove from heat.
2. Add baking soda, and vanilla. Mix well.
3. Pour evenly over popped corn and mix until corn is uniformly covered.
4. Place in a large disposable aluminum pan or large roaster.
5. Bake at 225°F for 1 hr. Stir every 15 minutes.
6. Store in air-tight containers.
7. Serve as an appetizer or snack.

Baked Acorn Squash

1 acorn squash
2 T butter
salt and pepper to taste
brown sugar to taste

1. Cut squash in half, remove seeds and wash the outside thoroughly.
2. Place butter in each half.
3. Wrap each half in aluminum foil.
4. Place a rack inside a crock pot or slow cooker. Add 1" of water. Place squash on the rack, inside up.
5. Cook covered on low for 7-8 hours or until done.
6. Remove from cooker and unwrap foil.
7. Add salt, pepper and/or brown sugar to taste as desired.
8. Serve.

Serves 2 per squash.

Deb's Pineapple-Cherry Tidbits

1 fresh pineapple
1 ¼ c white sugar
½ c brown sugar
½ tsp cinnamon
maraschino cherries, large, halved
toothpicks

1. Remove outside layer of pineapple; core. Cut pineapple into slices and then cut slices into bite-sized pieces as shown above.
2. In a bowl, mix sugars and cinnamon. Dip pineapple pieces in mixture; then place pieces on a parchment-lined baking sheet.
3. Place a maraschino cherry half on each pineapple slice.
4. Place baking sheet under a broiler for 4-6 minutes or until pineapple surface is bubbly.
5. Remove from oven and place a toothpick through each pineapple-cherry piece.

This is like having a pineapple upside down cake without the cake! They may be used as a light dessert or as an appetizer.

Deb

Gingerbread House

Follow the recipe for Gingerbread Men Cookies; it will make enough dough for a small house. H.

<u>Royal Icing</u>
4 c confectioner's sugar, sifted
3 T Wilton meringue powder
5 T water

1. In a large bowl, using a stand mixer, beat ingredients at medium speed for 7-10 minutes or until icing forms peaks and loses sheen. (If using a hand mixer, mix for 10-12 minutes.)

Note: Beat longer and at increased speed if peaks don't form.

<u>House</u>
1. Check Google for size directions.
2. Use your imagination while decorating house with assorted candies.

INDEX

Appetizers	pp. 3
Brie en Croute	pp. 8-9
Crab Tartlet with Lemon-Dill Sauce	pp. 4-5
Fruit Dip	pp. 7
Jalapeno Peppers	pp. 6
Soups	pp. 10
Baked Potato Soup	pp. 11
Butternut Squash Soup	pp. 15
Chili	pp. 12
Ham and Bean Soup	pp. 14
Taco Soup	pp. 13
Salads	pp. 16
Crab Salad Pasta	pp. 27
Cranberry Pineapple Salad	pp. 24
Orange Sprinkle Salad	pp. 17
Patriotic Jell-O Salad	pp. 20-21
Pineapple Chicken Salad Sandwiches	pp. 25
Potato Salad	pp. 26
Pretzel Salad	pp. 22-23
Seven Layer Salad	pp. 18-19
Breads	pp. 28
Best Ever Banana Nut Bread	pp. 36
Beverly's Chicken Croquettes	pp. 29
Cheese Braid Coffee Cake	pp. 34-35
Chocolate Zucchini Bread	pp. 37
Cinnamon Rolls	pp. 42-43
Easy Waffles	pp. 40
Elegant Swan Lemon Cream Puffs	pp. 38-39

Raisin Bran Muffins — pp. 41
Refrigerator Potato Rolls — pp. 32-33
Swedish Tea Ring — pp. 30-31

Casseroles — pp. 44
Baked Corn Casserole — pp. 46
Chicken Pot Pie — pp. 52-53
Eggplant Casserole — pp. 56-57
Fourth of July Bean Casserole — pp. 47
Glenda's Amish Breakfast Casserole — pp. 45
Hash Brown Casserole — pp. 58
Reuben Crescent Bake — pp. 50-51
Spaghetti Pie — pp. 48-49
Steak Pot Pie — pp. 54-55

Entrees — pp. 59
Baked Chicken Salad Wreath — pp. 66
Citrus Sauce Pork Chops — pp. 60-61
Garden Fresh Stromboli Rolls — pp. 64-65
Peperoni Spinach Quiche — pp. 62-63
Ruthie's Meat Loaf — pp. 67

Desserts — pp. 68-126
Amish Brown Sugar Dumplings — pp. 108-109
Amish Buttermilk Cookies — pp. 86-87
Amish Date-Nut Pudding — pp. 110-111
Apple Crisp — pp. 106
Apple Dumplings — pp. 118-119
Bread Pudding — pp. 107
Buckeyes — pp. 102-103
Butter Horns — pp. 92-93
Butter Pie Crust — pp. 114
Butterscotch Pie — pp. 125
Carrot Cake — pp. 70-71
Clothespin Cookies — pp. 100-101
Classic Crisco Pie Crust — pp. 115
Deluxe Oatmeal Cookies — pp. 88-89

Earthquake Cake	pp. 76-77
Elegant Chocolate Torte	pp. 80-81
Fresh Black Raspberry Pie	pp. 120-121
Gingerbread Men Cookies	pp. 90-91
Hummingbird Cake	pp. 74-75
Key Lime Cake	pp. 72-73
Lemon Meringue Pie	pp. 126
Libby Pumpkin Pie	pp. 117
Linda's Chocolate Cake	pp. 82
Linda's Chocolate Cake Icing	pp. 83
Meringue	pp. 124
Pecan Tarts	pp. 94-95
Peppermint Patty Sandwich Cookies	pp. 96-97
Philly Cream Cheese Frosting	pp 69
Royal Icing	pp. 135
Strawberry Cookies	pp. 84-85
Strawberry Rhubarb Pie	pp. 116
Sugar Cookies	pp. 98-99
Triple Nut Diamond Cookies	pp. 104-105
Vanilla Pudding	pp. 112-113
Washington State Apple Pie	pp. 122-123
Woolworth's Icebox Cheese Cake	pp. 78-79
Miscellaneous	pp. 127
Baked Acorn Squash	pp, 133
Caramel Corn	pp. 132
Club Rollups	pp. 129
Deb's Pineapple-Cherry Tidbits	pp. 134
Fruit Pizza	pp. 130-131
Gingerbread House	pp. 135
Veggie Pizza	pp. 128
Index	pp. 136
Acknowledgements	pp. 139

Acknowledgements

Making a recipe book for my family is a long-time dream of mine. I am grateful for my special friend, JoAnn Quitmeyer, who has helped make my dream come true. Her endless hours of typing and editing have been a labor of love and selflessness and I can never thank her enough.

I also want to thank my God-given family and friends, many whom have encouraged me to achieve this goal at my age and at this stage of my life. With their support, my dream has come true. My family will be surprised.

God has given me the abilities to refine these cooking and baking skills over the years. He has given me many opportunities to share these gifts with countless family members and friends. He has allowed me to use these abilities to be a blessing and to bring His love to others in a tangible and delicious way. I am thankful!

H.

Enjoy!

H.

www.ingramcontent.com/pod-product-compliance
Lightning Source LLC
Chambersburg PA
CBHW082105280426
43661CB00089B/866